CRYSTAL RUNES

ELLA MORTIMER

Second Edition © Copyright Ella Mortimer 2017

ISBN-13: 978-0-6482320-4-9

No part of this publication may be reproduced, stored in a retrieval system, or transmitted in any form or by any means, electronic, mechanical, photocopying, recording or otherwise, without the prior permission of the author, nor be circulated in any binding or cover other than that in which it is published.

All places and characters in this book are fictitious and any resemblance to actual places or persons, living or dead, are purely coincidental.

Previously published in 2014 under the pseudonym Ella Stradling. Sharon Ella Mortimer asserts the moral right to be identified as the author of this work and retains all rights to and ownership of this work.

Amenti Books is a trademark shared by individual entities trading independently in an unincorporated joint venture. Amenti Books does not trade independently and is not a legal entity for tax purposes.

Manuscript © Sharon Ella Mortimer 2014
First Edition ISBN 978 1495458262
Kindle Edition ASIN B075FTMV35

Cover Art © S. E. Mortimer, using her own work and commercial license images from daisytrail.com.

A catalogue record for this book is available from the National Library of Australia.

theraceoffire.amentibooks.com

QUICK KEY

Physical	Emotional	Spiritual
FEE Authority — Onyx	 **HAIL** Disruption — Snowflake Obsidian	 **TRY** Fighting — Red Jasper
 **RAW** Freedom — Haematite	 **NEED** Necessity — Tiger Iron	 **BIRTH** Loving — Unakite
 **THORN** Chaos — Flourite	 **ICE** Hibernation — Amethyst	 **WAY** Vehicle — Sodalite
 **VOICE** Wisdom — Agate	**YEAR** Growth — Aventurine	 **MAN** Driver — Clear Quartz
 **RIDE** Journey — Calcite	 **BOW** Vigilance — Rhodonite	 **LAGOON** Preparation — Moonstone
 **CANDLE** Beacon — Nephrite	**PEAR** Indulgence — Malachite	 **SPRING** Completion — Moss Agate
 **GIVE** Giving — Rose Quartz	 **SHIELD** Retreat — Bloodstone	 **ETHOS** History — Fossilised Wood
WIN Winning — Carnelian	 **SIGNAL** Advance — Citrine	**DAY** Today — Chalcedony

CONTENTS

About the Runes..... 1
Making the Runes... 7
    Stone Runes 8
    Wooden Runes .. 14
    Clay Runes 16
    Found Runes 18
    Card Runes....... 20
Casting the Runes 27
    One Rune.......... 28
    Three Times 29
    Four Seasons 32
    Five Fingers 36
    Six Senses 40
    Seven Chakras.. 44
    Fee Says 48
    Hail Says 51
    Try Says............ 54
Reading the Runes 57
    Fee.................... 58
    Raw 62
    Thorn................ 66

Voice................. 70
Ride 74
Candle 78
Give 82
Win.................... 86
Hail.................... 90
Need 94
Ice..................... 98
Year 102
Bow 106
Pear 110
Shield 114
Signal 118
Try................... 122
Birth 126
Way 130
Lagoon 138
Spring............. 142
Ethos 146
Day 150

ABOUT THE RUNES

ELLA MORTIMER

I first came across the Viking runes some twenty years ago, and quickly became enamoured of them. But, like many beginners, I never explored past the one text supplied with my commercially bought set. So it was that years passed before I realised the meanings to which I had grown so accustomed might not be particularly accurate. This is not to say they were any less relevant, but they were one person's well-considered interpretation. The author of that set had their own personal reasons for creating that particular text.

Finally, I grew enough in my experience to break away, and explore other ideas. I learnt about the original structure and meanings of the runes, and their complicated history. I discovered that in creating the text I had first used, that author had changed the order of the runes, breaking the traditional structure and imposing their own, new interpretation on the very fabric of the runic system of divination.

I began to wonder what else had changed over the centuries, through so many explorations, by so many practitioners. I found that even the basic meanings had been influenced by second hand interpretations. And the simple, worldly advice of the runes had been diluted by intense spiritual interpretations, taking them away from the practical intent conveyed in the earliest writings.

I wanted to return to the original meanings, approaching it as an academic study, to discover the runes in their purest form. I wanted to return to the source, without being overshadowed by so many other people's ideas. In short, I wanted my own set, following the original rules, which would be taken directly from the very earliest runic texts.

Little did I realise that my quest would take me five years, and that only after authoring five novels would I be ready to begin writing my personal interpretation of the Anglo-Saxon (not Viking) runes.

The use of runes for divination is first documented by the Roman historian Tacitus in his descriptions of Celtic worship. The first runic inscriptions appear in the third century. This "Elder Futhark" script developed among the Germanic tribes of Europe, in its earliest form of twenty-four characters.

In Britain the futhark was adapted and expanded to thirty-three characters to accomodate the Anglo-Saxon language. This script was picked up by the Vikings and taken back to Scandinavia, where it was again adapted, and the list was shortened to sixteen characters to become what is known as the "Younger Futhark".

The earliest surviving rune poem, listing the rune names and meanings, is written in Anglo-Saxon (Old) English, and was followed by two later Scandinavian poems. The Icelandic and Nordic poems contain fewer runes, but follow the same basic meanings, more or less.

ELLA MORTIMER

It is thought that the extra characters in the Anglo-Saxon poem were added as the English language developed, and the oldest engravings do support this theory. Modern rune sets generally follow the Elder Futhark collection of twenty-four runes, regardless of whether the author has chosen to use runic names from the Anglo-Saxon record or Proto-Germanic names, which are a linguistic best-guess of a supposed parent dialect from which all Germanic languages evolved.

My personal preference for Anglo-Saxon names comes more from an affinity to the language than any belief that those names are more accurate. In fact, my first introduction to the runes involved the Proto-Germanic names. But in the Anglo-Saxon, many of the names are still recognisable in modern English, if you can find the right modern word.

I have chosen to give each rune a modern keyword for its name, to reflect both the original Anglo-Saxon word and its meaning. In so doing, I have found not only the rune names easier to remember, but the divinations as well. It is not a change of name, but rather a translation that brings them into our modern language.

The original structure of the runes followed two distinct rules. First is the three internal divisions known as Aettir. Each Aet consists of eight runes (Aet, eight, you see how the language survives). Headed by the rune of its patron god, each Aet is influenced by one

CRYSTAL RUNES

aspect of life: physical, emotional and spiritual.

The second internal structure is the runic pairs. Each rune is followed by its pair, which is an opposite or complement of the rune it follows. I have chosen main keywords to reflect this structure. These words take the meaning of the rune to its divinatory conclusion, while enhancing the connection between the pairs.

On the facing pages, I have quoted the Anglo-Saxon rune poem, using my own poetic translation, as an introduction to the runic interpretations. In every case, especially when there is a popular discrepancy of meaning, I have returned to this poem for my interpretation.

On the pages following each rune page, you will find a list of keywords to further clarify the meaning. These are followed by in-depth descriptions of the runes, incorporating all the translated meanings, keywords, interpretations and in some cases explanation of the research behind the choices made.

In this book, each rune is paired with a semi-precious stone. I have long held a fascination for crystals and their healing powers, and in this rune set I have combined the runes with the power of crystals to enhance your readings. Each stone has been chosen to complement the divinatory meaning of the rune, giving the reader the opportunity to use the stone in meditation or simply as a further point of discussion within the reading.

The stones are not included with this book,

but there are instructions for creating your own set, or you may cut out and use the cards provided in the chapter Making the Runes. Cut out or copy them and place them face down on the table. Swirl them about with your hands and select your cards at random, laying them out in one of the spreads in the chapter Casting the Runes. If you make your own stones, you might like to also make a small bag in which to keep them, and draw them out of your bag one at a time.

    When you have your runes ready, turn to the chapter Casting the Runes and read the spreads described there. Beginning with the most simple runic spreads and progressing to more complex, it is important that you consider carefully which spread might be most helpful for your current question. Examine each position described in your chosen spread before you attempt to draw your runes, then draw out your runes in the order described for your chosen spread and lay them out as pictured, then read the interpretations from Reading the Runes. Use both the position descriptions and the runic interpretations together to divine your answers. Good luck, and have lots of fun!

MAKING THE RUNES

STONE RUNES

CRYSTAL RUNES

There are many ways to create a rune set. The earliest runes were carved on twigs. Many commercial sets are available, some made from clay or a similar man-made substance, some made from stones of some kind.

This book is designed to be used with crystals, each stone selected for its affinity with the rune inscribed upon it. However, these interpretations can be used with any set you care to choose, or make yourself. A hand-made set can be particularly effective, as your own spiritual essence is infused into your set by the act of creation.

You may use any runes you like with this book, but if you wish to create your own crystal runes to use, follow the instructions below.

Here listed are the crystals I have selected for each rune. Most of these should be easily found by any reasonable crystal supplier, or ordered from your nearest "new age" store.

Ideally you want tumbled stones of between 2cm and 4cm diameter. Any smaller and the power of the stones is too much reduced, and they are fiddly to draw out of your bag. Any larger and they become cumbersome and difficult to hold comfortably, not to mention heavy. You want stones that sit nicely in the palm of your hand.

The rune symbols can be painted or engraved onto each stone. If you intend to engrave your stones, be careful of stones with inner flaws, as these may crack or shatter. If you decide to paint them, or use indelible pens, you may need to re-paint occasionally, as the rubbing action inside the rune bag will scratch the paint away (some markers can be set by baking the stones in the oven). I have had great success painting the runes with nail polish!

Just find all the stones on the list and create your set. Please note: names of crystals tend to change over the years. I have provided a brief description and wherever possible I have noted these alternate names. I have also included alternate stones you can use if you can't find or don't like a particular stone.

Fee = Onyx - Generally black, with or without layers of white or translucent stone. Lately marketed as "Black Agate". Alternate Stones: Moonstone, Amethyst.

Raw = Haematite - Metallic grey to silver, can be magnetised and used in magnetic jewellery. Sometimes called "Bloodstone" or "Magnetite". Alternate Stones: Bloodstone, Abstract Jasper.

Thorn = Flourite - A variety of quartz with variations of colour, usually blue, green, clear and purple. Sometimes called "Rainbow Flourite", especially if there are more quartz colours in the mix. Alternate Stones: Onyx, Turquoise.

Voice = Agate - Bands of colour, usually in pale browns and whites. Often dyed in bright colours. Also called "Banded Agate". Alternate Stones: Amazonite, Moonstone.

CRYSTAL RUNES

Ride = Yellow Calcite - Translucent yellow, usually with a cloudy, slightly iridescent quality. Often not as highly polished as other tumbled stones. May be called "Honey Calcite". Alternate Stones: Dalmation Jasper, Mookaite.

Candle = Nephrite Jade - Soft jade green with white blotchy patches. Could be sold as "Nephrite" or "Jadeite". Alternate Stones: Garnet, Tourmaline.

Give = Rose Quartz - Pale pink translucent stone from the quartz family. Alternate Stones: Carnelian, Malachite.

Win = Carnelian - Dark yellow to deep orange and brown in bands of colour, sometimes with layers of translucent yellow or opaque cream. Alternate Stones: Red Jasper, Aventurine.

Hail = Snowflake Obsidian - Black with greyish white spots or blotches throughout. Alternate Stones: Onyx, Tourmaline.

Need = Tiger Iron - Layers of browns and creams with highly iridescent bands of a golden colour. You could substitute "Tiger's Eye", "Iron Tiger Eye", or one of many other market names. Alternate Stones: Amazonite, Unakite.

Ice = Amethyst - A form of quartz with pale to deep purple colouring with a pronounced crystalline structure. Sometimes with inclusions of white. Alternate Stones: Blue Quartz, Moonstone.

ELLA MORTIMER

Year = Aventurine - Translucent jade green stone with a grainy appearance. Sometimes called "Green Quartz". Alternate Stones: Yellow Jasper, Amazonite.

Bow = Rhodonite - Pink with blotchy inclusions of dark grey to black. Alternate Stones: Bloodstone, Crazy Lace Agate.

Pear = Malachite - Shades of bright to dark green in bands of colour. Alternate Stones: Opal, Red Jasper.

Shield = Heliotrope - Dark green with blotchy inclusions of rusty red. Sometimes called "Bloodstone" or "Green Jasper". Alternate Stones: Abstract Jasper, Tiger Eye.

Signal = Citrine - Transparent yellow, a yellow form of quartz. May be called "Citrine Quartz" or "Yellow Quartz". Alternate Stones: Yellow Calcite, Tiger Iron.

Try = Red Jasper - Opaque rusty red, sometimes with inclusions. There are many varieties of jasper. For this set try for something predominantly red. Alternate Stones: Haematite, Amazonite.

Birth = Unakite - Streaks of green and light brown in various shades. Also known as "Epidote". Alternate Stones: Aventurine, Moss Agate.

Way = Sodalite - Deep blue with swirls and streaks and blotches of white. Alternate Stones: Crazy Lace Agate, Mookaite.

CRYSTAL RUNES

Man = Clear Quartz - Clear, colourless, transparent stone, sometimes with crystalline structures or fractures, and occasionally with inclusions of white. Sometimes called "Rock Crystal". Alternate Stones: Turquoise, Onyx.

Lagoon = Moonstone - Creamy white to pale brownish cream, opaque to translucent, with iridescent qualities. Lately the most available form is sold as "Rainbow Moonstone". Alternate Stones: Banded Agate, Blue Quartz.

Spring = Moss Agate - Blotchy green and white, with occasional brownish inclusions. Alternate Stones: Green Jasper, Rutilated Quartz.

Ethos = Fossilised wood - Brownish bands, varying from white to grey to brown. Also known as "Petrified Wood". Alternate Stones: Dalmation Jasper, Rhyolite.

Day = Chalcedony - Many stones come from the chalcedony family, but the one required here is the blue form. Bands of colour from white to pale blue and mid blue. Sometimes called "Blue Chalcedony" or "Blue Agate". Be careful of agate that has been dyed blue, which is not the same stone. Alternate Stones: Clear Quartz, Sodalite.

WOODEN RUNES

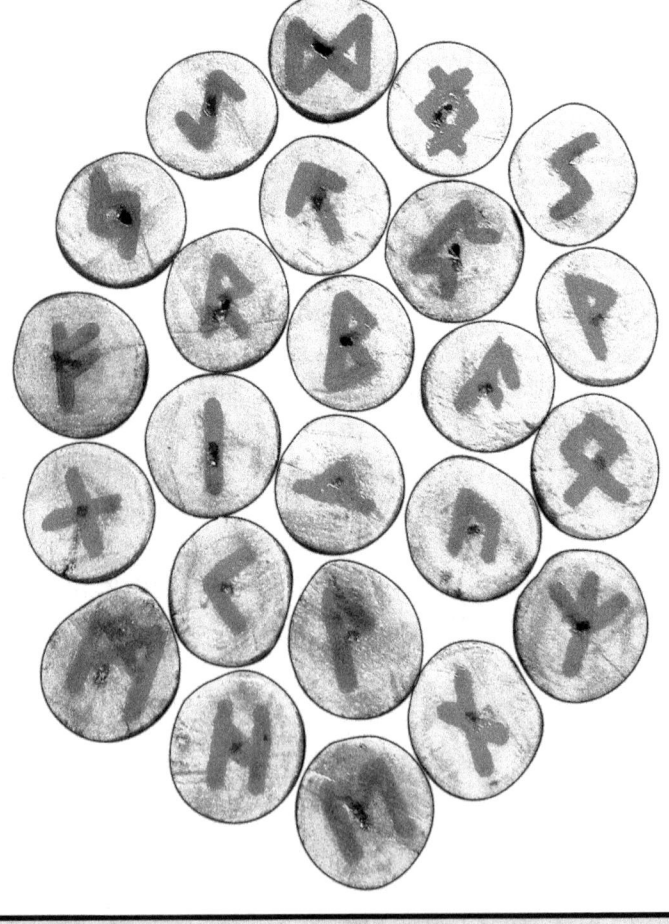

CRYSTAL RUNES

One of the easiest ways to make your own runes is to use twigs or a branch from your own garden. The earliest forms are described as twigs cut into short lengths with symbols carved into the bark. An especially pleasing method is to find a fairly thick branch and cut it into rounds, then carve or burn the runes into the round face.

I made the set pictured from a eucalyptus branch, about 15mm thick, cut into rounds and sanded. These are a delightfully dainty set, very lightweight and pleasant to hold, and full of natural energy.

The runes were drawn with a red marker pen and the rounds varnished with sparkly nail polish. Which proves you don't need any special equipment or expensive supplies to make your runes. In fact, the more home-made the better.

CLAY RUNES

CRYSTAL RUNES

Many modern commercial rune sets are made by creating a clay mold and casting the stones in polystone or another toughened man-made ceramic. This produces a set that appears to be "made from the earth", but it is an illusion. There is nothing wrong with these sets, but what about making your own from clay?

Imagine the feel of the clay, the joy of molding them with your own hands and carving the runes into the wet stones, then baking them yourself. Or, if you don't have access to real clay, try modelling clay!

A few years ago there were a lot of hand-made beads appearing on market stalls made from a kind of modelling clay which could be molded and then baked, that could be any colour you like, or mixed together to make a swirl of colour. The set pictured was made from my daughter's play-dough, left to dry hard on its own.

FOUND RUNES

CRYSTAL RUNES

What else do you think would make good rune stones? Many ancient cultures placed a lot of spiritual value on found objects, things that you pick up and keep in a special pouch and carry as talismans.

You could collect river pebbles and engrave them. Or you could collect crystals of all the same kind, as some commercial sets are. You could buy some pebbles of soapstone, which is easy to carve and can even be surface dyed before carving so the symbols stand out when you carve through the dye to the white soapstone below.

In Australia, quite some years ago, we stopped using our copper 1c and 2c coins. Many people still have a little collection of these now worthless coins. Can you imagine a handful of copper coins, polished to a burnished gold and inscribed with runes?

You could experiment with papiér maché. Perhaps some colourful beads, or some other found object. What about ceramic tiles? The delightful set pictured are made from thick glass tesserae, of the type you might find in a garden store or a cheap variety store. Let your imagination decide.

CARD RUNES

FEE

RAW

THORN
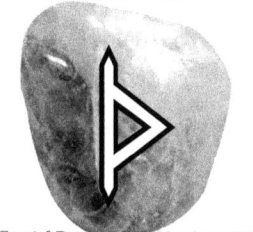

VOICE

RIDE

CANDLE
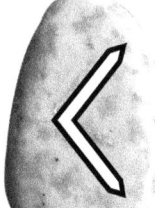

GIVE

WIN

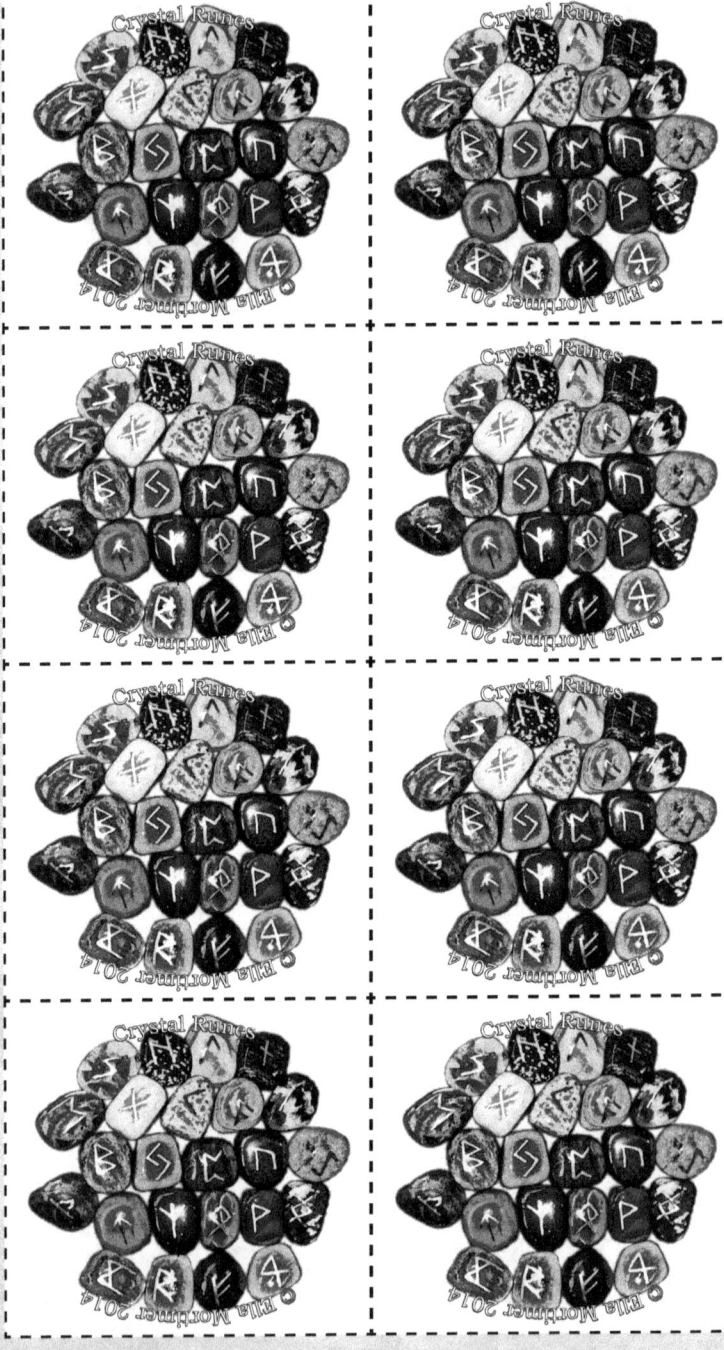

HAIL

NEED

ICE

YEAR

BOW

PEAR

SHIELD

SIGNAL

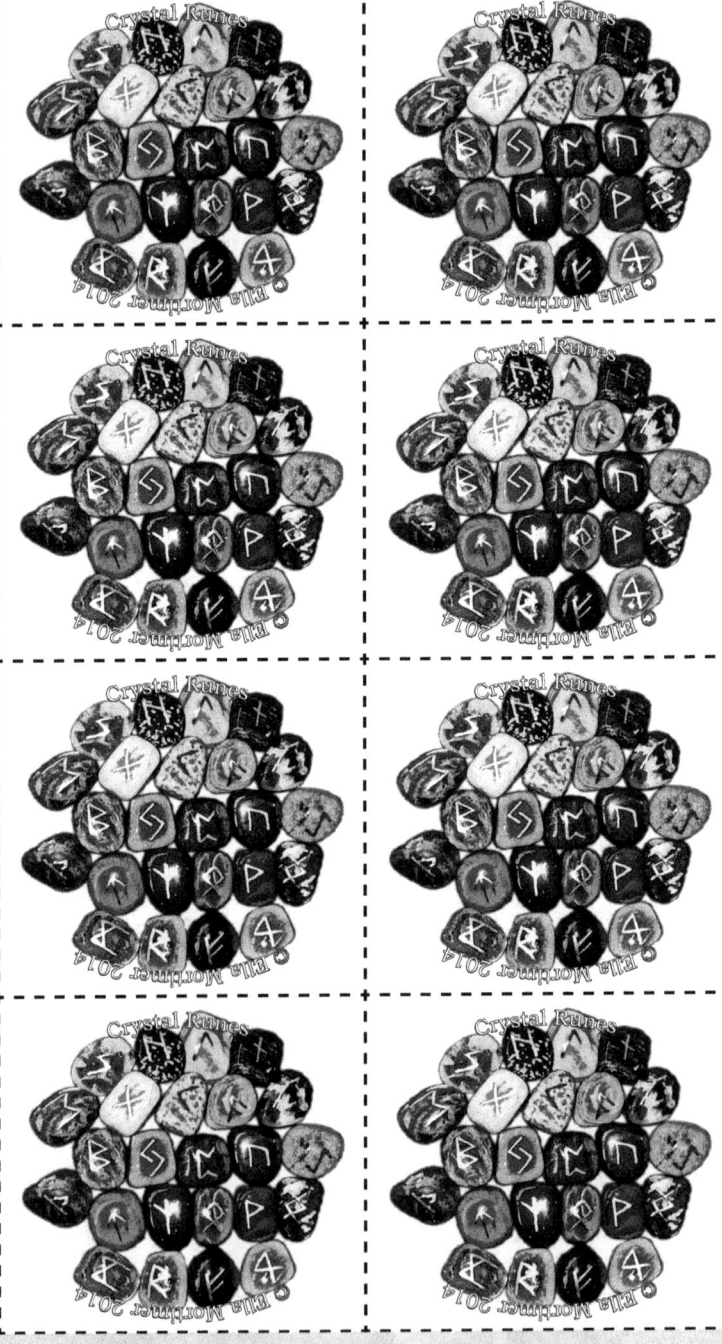

TRY 	**BIRTH** 
WAY 	**MAN** 
LAGOON 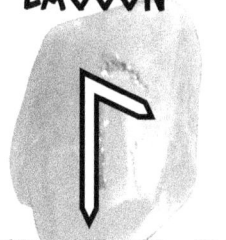	**SPRING** 
ETHOS 	**DAY** 

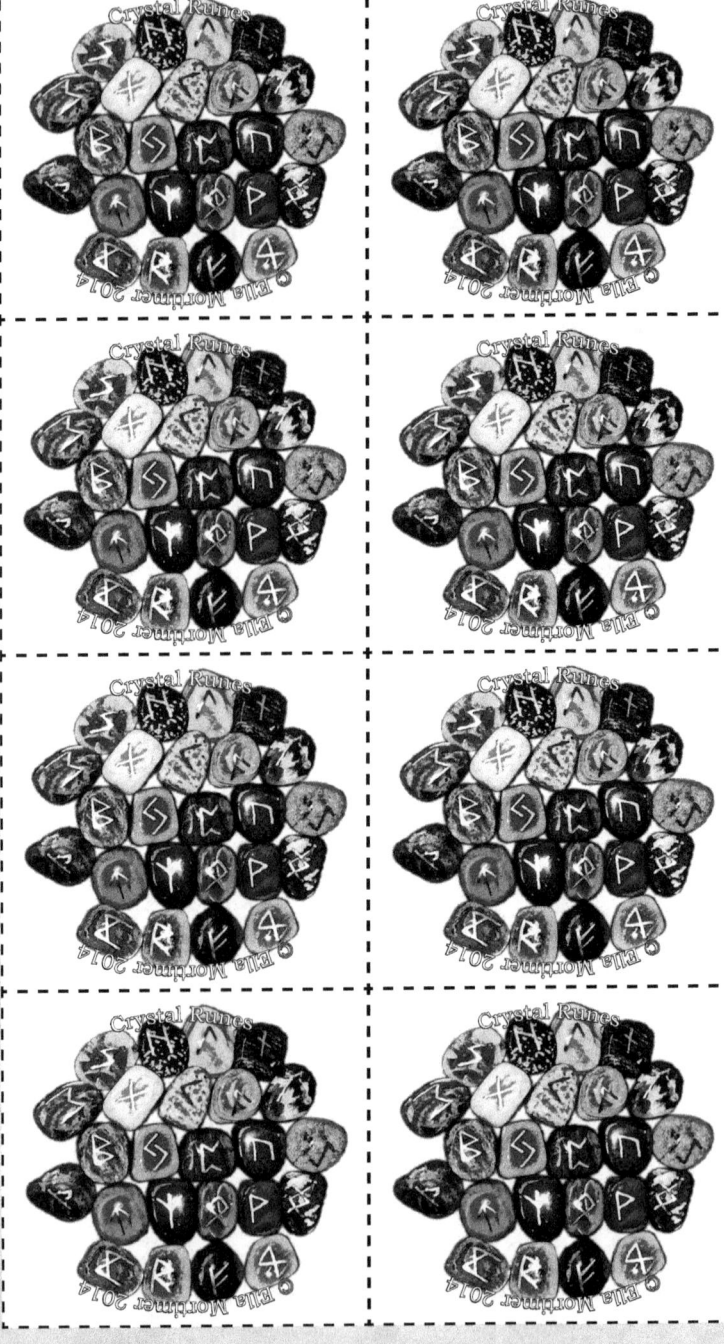

ONE RUNE

The Comment

1. The comment

Perhaps the most simple of all runic divination methods, the single rune can also be the most helpful, and has the potential to become the most used method in your daily life. You may want to use it every day, by drawing it as a pointer for that day, or you may want to use it only at times when you require a quick, one aspect answer.

Draw out one rune only, then take the meaning as a comment, or an answer. You may choose to simply read the one-word translation and take what meaning you will from that, or you may like to read the whole interpretation as laid out in this book. Either way, it is a quick, easy method in today's fast-paced world.

THREE TIMES

Past **Present** **Future**

If you are looking for something slightly more revealing, yet still in a quick, easy reading, try the three times spread.

This popular spread is found in many divination systems, under various names, and is useful if you require a comment on cause and effect, on the circumstances that led to your current question and the possible outcome.

Read the meanings of the positions on the following page. Reach into your bag and draw out three runes, one at a time, thinking of your question and that rune's position in the spread, and lay them down in the order indicated in the illustration.

Then read their meanings in consideration of the position in which they fall.

ELLA MORTIMER

1. The past

This position indicates the events or actions that led to your current situation, or the forces at play behind the question you have asked.

These influences have already occurred, so they cannot be changed, but they can guide you toward a reason for your present situation. Take the interpretation of the rune drawn as an indication of what needs to be changed or resolved.

2. The present

This aspect tells you where you are now, what problem faces you at this time, or what lies at the heart of your question. Use the rune meaning to shine a light on what may be troubling you or causing your current problem.

Think of it as illumination, something to give you a light in the darkness, providing clarity so that you may move forward and resolve the matter, or perhaps vanquish your demons.

Conversely, it may show you what you are doing right. It may be an affirmation, the reassurance that you are taking the correct path, offering confidence to continue on your present course.

3. The future

This rune will tell you where you might find yourself if you follow the advice of the second position, or may warn of the outcome if you do

CRYSTAL RUNES

not.

It may be that the advice you received from the second rune required no action, in which case, this is the future situation you can not avoid.

In any case, it is not set in stone. Your actions in the present will determine the outcome. If this position appears dire, change your thinking and find a way to avoid it.

If it appears positive, take your cue from the present and embrace the future.

FOUR SEASONS

Winter

Autumn

Spring

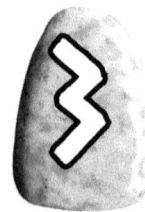

Summer

This spread is useful if you seek advice over the long term. As suggested by the title and names of the positions, this spread is intended to cover a full calendar year, but the seasons do not necessarily coincide with the actual seasons of the year.

Consider the positions in a divinatory light, describing the progression of your situation, beginning in the deep winter of doubt, giving way to the spring that will pull you from the cold and the summer of a successful outcome, followed by the autumn of rest and rebuilding.

Of course, there is always the chance that these aspects seem to indicate the reverse, but if this occurs consider them in the light of the advice they give. Sometimes a backwards progression may be offering a choice, giving warning of what may happen if you continue in your present course. In this case, try to modify your actions accordingly, and try the spread again in three months' time.

1. Winter

This position involves the deepest aspect of your current problem or question, the very heart of the matter at hand. It will tell you how you are affected by your current situation and what is holding you back. It does not look back at how you got here, but only why you are stuck here. The past is gone, and this is the present, and you need to recognise where you are to consider what you must do.

2. Spring

Just as the winter must eventually give way to the thaw and spring must burst forth, so must your problem be resolved by right action. This position tells you what you need in order to pull yourself out of winter and into the new growth of spring. New growth that will lead you out of your problem and take you toward a successful outcome. Take the advice of the rune that falls in this position, and begin to build your new beginning.

3. Summer

This is the happy outcome, the hoped for conclusion, the best that can happen if you follow the advice given by the rune of spring. If this rune appears negative, take it as a warning of what may happen if you do not take the steps required.

Conversely, perhaps a seemingly poor outcome has a silver lining, perhaps the outcome is what you really need. Summer is a time of nurture, of raising offspring when the new birth has already come.

Think of the flower that has already dropped its petals to feed the growing seed. Try to read deeper, search within, find the seed of new life already growing within.

4. Autumn

A time of taking stock, of gathering resources and reflecting on the year that has passed. This position warns that no success is without danger, that life is a cycle just as are the seasons of the year. There will always be bad times with the good, and a successful outcome is not a time to rest.

People have always used the bounty of summer to provide sustenance during the cold of winter. This rune will tell you what you need to learn from your time of travail, so that your next task will be easier. Reflect on lessons learnt, and build for the times to come.

FIVE FINGERS

Pinky

Ringman

Tallman

Thumb

Pointer

CRYSTAL RUNES

I considered naming this spread five aspects, rather than fingers, but I wanted to show the character of each position, which make up one whole situation. Each finger has a specific function, each giving its unique contribution to the inner structure of the hand.

If you want to delve into the aspects of your problem, to understand it without necessarily finding the solution, this is your spread.

1. Pinky

The smallest and cutest finger, and the one most commonly overlooked. It sits there at the edge of the hand, seemingly unused. But have you considered life without it?

This position indicates the little things, the things we overlook. Every problem has little aspects, working away behind the scenes, hiding in plain sight and adding up, becoming the building blocks of the big picture.

Use this rune to find the little things that you may have failed to see.

2. Ringman

This finger is filled with symbolism, carried down through the ages, the ring finger, the most revered position. It indicates the part of the problem you are holding in your heart, the one aspect you cherish without realising it is in fact the most important.

Not the ringman, but the ring leader or ring master. The aspect of the problem that gathers all the others to it while commanding your devoted attention. Use this rune to discover that part of the problem you must give up, the sacrifice you must make.

3. Tallman

The longest finger, the one with the most reach. In recent years, taking on the persona of the "rude" finger. Think of this as the tail of the dog, waggling there, drawing your gaze while taking your attention away from the real problem.

It is the most reactionary position, the part of the problem that is making you act out of character, drawing the gaze of others. It is the position behind which you hide the truth of your problem.

This rune will help you see yourself from the perspective of an outsider, showing you what others see of you.

4. Pointer

Your index finger is the strongest and most used. It points the way, it pulls the trigger, it swipes the touch-screen. This position shows you the most powerful aspect of your problem, the aspect with the most influence on your situation.

Use the rune in this position to find the most important part of your problem, the aspect that will cause the most trouble. This is the true heart of the issue.

5. Thumb

It stands out, on its own while it rules over the others. Without the thumb, the hand would be just another foot. It is the digit that stands us apart from the crowd, allows us to grasp and use tools to better our lives.

In this position, consider the issue that controls everything. It touches all else, rounding them up and using them to make a fist. This rune will show you the biggest threat, the issue that keeps the others in line and holds them together to make one big problem. Break the thumb, and the whole hand falls apart.

SIX SENSES

Thought

Sound

Sight

Touch

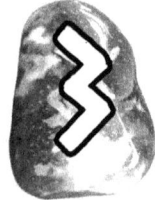
Smell

Taste

CRYSTAL RUNES

Sometimes, all you need is a way to examine the issue, advice to help you come to some decision on your own.

The six senses spread is designed to break up your question and delineate the ways in which it affects you personally, highlighting the issue through your own perception of the problem. This will give insight into the emotional and physical consequences and how to combat them.

If you want to delve deep into yourself, or if you need help to make a decision, try this spread.

1. Sight

This position relates to how you view the question, what you think is the main issue and the solution as you see it. Are you seeing it right?

Use this rune to help you see more clearly. It may offer advice on the way forward or help you to change your perspective to see it in a different light.

2. Sound

In this position, your rune will help you hear the message inherent in the situation. No problem or decision is clear cut, and sometimes these questions plague us for a reason. There is something you need to learn, or something your doubt is trying to tell you. Use this rune to amplify the sound and decipher the message.

3. Smell

Sometimes smell can be the first indication of a problem. The smell of smoke heralds fire, and we all know the odour of rotting fruit. How many times have you taken the milk out of the 'fridge and smelt it to see if it's alright to drink?

Use this rune as your early warning, your first whiff of a problem, and take appropriate action. Or, take the time to smell the roses.

4. Taste

When you open your mouth and take something in, how does it taste? Is it sweet, sour, or salty? Or does it taste bad? What would your problem's solution taste like?

It sounds simple, but sometimes that is the change in perspective you need. Sometimes taste is a warning. Use this rune to discover how your question tastes on your spiritual tongue.

5. Touch

What does the question feel like? Take hold of it, play with it, let your spiritual fingers explore it. Is it rough, smooth, a little soft, or wet?

This rune will give you the feel of the problem, showing you a visceral reaction that you might not have considered before. Perhaps this new perspective can help you make your decision.

6. Thought

The mythical sixth sense is the ability to know through psychic means. In this position, you can look at your problem through your spiritual self, using the power of intuition.

On a personal level, this is your internal dialogue, what you tell yourself about the issue. Sometimes our internal voice is wrong. This rune will show you what you are saying to yourself.

Crown

Third Eye

Throat

Heart

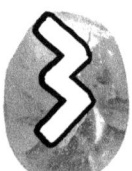
Naval

Sacral

SEVEN CHAKRAS

Root

CRYSTAL RUNES

One aspect of Hindu teaching that has been widely adopted by spiritual practitioners the world over is the concept of energy centres called chakras. These wheels of energy exist along the line of the spine from base to crown, each governing certain aspects of human awareness.

An imbalance in one or more of these energy centres can cause problems on mental, spiritual, emotional and physical levels. The seven chakras spread is designed for those times when you feel generally out of balance for no particular reason.

This spread will help you determine where you may be experiencing imbalance or blockage, and how to correct it. It is advised to pay special attention if the crystal rune matches the colour of the chakra position in which it is drawn.

1. Root

The root chakra is located at the base of the spine. Ruled by the colour red, its element is Earth. It is the centre of fear, reproduction and physical need. It governs all the most basic, instinctual desires of human existence.

The rune in this position will give you an insight into your primitive self, and offer advice for correction of any imbalance you may be experiencing in this aspect of life.

2. Sacral

The sacral chakra is located low in the stomach, below the naval. Its colour is orange and its element is water. Its ruling emotion is desire, governing all aspects of sensual pleasure and feeling.

The rune in this position will point to any disharmony in the areas of intimacy, sexual dysfunction or relationships.

3. Navel

The third chakra is the navel, located over that region of the body known as the solar plexus. It is yellow, with the ruling element of fire. Physically, it governs the digestive system.

This position relates to energy and inner strength. This rune will point to any weakness in self control, or loss of vitality, and offer advice for correcting any imbalance.

4. Heart

The heart chakra governs love and self-esteem, compassion and the ability to forgive. Its colour is green and its ruling element is air. It regulates the heart and lungs and generates trust and sharing.

The rune in this position will indicate any problems with these areas of emotional stability, and offer methods for coping with life and generating new ideas.

5. Throat

Located at the neck, the throat chakra is blue. Its element is ether, and it governs speech, communication and creativity. Any problems in these areas will be made apparent by the rune drawn in this position.

Meditating on the message offered will bring clarity and a feeling of openness, with a strengthening of the life force.

6. Third eye

The sixth chakra is located over the forehead, and is the energy centre for the third eye. As such, it governs all areas of intuition and understanding. Its colour is indigo and its element is light. Physically, it rules the eyes and the nervous system.

The rune in this position will help clear any blockage in the area of imagination, sixth sense and seeing the big picture.

7. Crown

The crown chakra is violet, and its element is thought. Located at the top of the head, the crown chakra governs all areas of wisdom, reason and spiritual awareness.

The rune in this position will help strengthen clarity of thought and higher consciousness, while offering ways to bring peace and harmony into your life.

Situation

Possessions

Home

Sustenance

Health

FEE SAYS

Outcome

CRYSTAL RUNES

The next three spreads will concentrate on one each of the three aettir, the three sets within the complete rune set, each ruled by the rune from which they take their name. Each spread is laid out in the shape of the ruling rune for that aet. This first spread concentrates on the physical world, ruled by the rune *Fee*.

1. Situation
The place in which you find yourself, and how it impacts on the world around you. This rune tells you the physical effect of the problem and how to counteract it.

2. Home
How is your question reflected in your home life and the people around you. This rune will help you see any imbalance at home that may be influencing your problem, and help you to find a way forward.

3. Possessions
This position concentrates on the material aspect of your question, pointing to the possessions you already have or those you may need to improve or solve your problem.

4. Health
This rune will point to your own personal space, your bodily health at the time of the question, and how it may be impacting on your problem.

5. Sustenance

The rune in this position will point to what you have that will sustain you in your quest or will give an indication of what you need to gain for a successful outcome.

6. Outcome

The most likely result if you are able to heed all the advice in the positions preceding this one. Alternatively, this position may give warning of the result if the conditions do not change.

HAIL SAYS

Situation

Requirement

Concern

Self

Sacrifice

Challenge

Impediment

Outcome

Movement

ELLA MORTIMER

Hail, the second aet, deals with situations of emotional health or distress. This spread will help you clarify any questions of doubt or pain caused either by a situation or a state of mind. This spread helps you look within, into your own emotional being.

1. Situation
The rune in this position will point to the emotional problem that is impacting your equilibrium. Consider the situation as it is highlighted by this rune.

2. Concern
This rune will help you see where the most pressing problem lies, giving insight into the deepest emotional aspect of your question.

3. Challenge
This position points to the emotional challenge ahead. It is only through testing that emotional growth can occur in order to solve the problem at hand.

4. Impediment
This rune will show you what stands in the way, preventing you from meeting the challenge. Take the advice of this rune to find a way forward.

5. Self
This rune steps back and takes a look at

you, through the eyes of the universe, to help you understand yourself in the light of your own emotional health. Consider this position as the friend telling you the truth to help you change and proceed.

6. Requirement
This position will show you what you must do. It does not tell you how to do it, but will show you the most important task, by finding that part of yourself that will help you work through your problem.

7. Sacrifice
Every emotional challenge requires a sacrifice. This is the aspect of your problem that you must give up, that part of yourself that is not required for the task at hand and is only hindering your progress.

8. Movement
This is the way forward, the action that will lead to your desired outcome. This rune acts as a signpost, indicating the way ahead.

9. Outcome
The outcome will depend on how you travel through your emotional journey. This position shows you the place you need to reach, but it is up to you to find it through diligence and hard work, following the advice laid out in this spread.

TRY SAYS

Meditation

Blockage

Options

Situation

Pathway

Opening

Solution

Outcome

CRYSTAL RUNES

The final aet follows the influence of *Try*, the rune of the warrior. This spread concentrates on the power of thought, the belief that you can and will reach your goals. It also involves higher thought, the spiritual realm and your own intuition.

1. Situation
The first position gives an insight into your problem and how it effects you spiritually and mentally. How your inner voice colours your perception of the problem.

2. Blockage
This rune will help you see where you are blocking yourself from forward movement. It is the outmoded thought that stops you solving the problem.

3. Meditation
This is the process of considering, the moment in which you discover the problem in all its phases. This rune will help you find an overall picture of the problem at hand.

4. Options
In order to move forward, you must explore all the possible paths and choose the most productive way forward. The rune in this position will help you see these various options and consider them.

5. Opening
This is the way forward. This rune will indicate the best path that will lead to your spiritual goal. Consider it as a doorway that you must choose to step through. Perhaps it will require a leap of faith.

6. Pathway
This is what lies beyond the door. If you choose to take this path, this rune will show you what you may expect. It will help you reconcile your inner voice to your spiritual goal and help you take that first step.

7. Solution
As you move forward, the path will become more clear. Your mind will become more calm and your confidence will grow as you strive toward your goal. This rune will give you the information you need to take the journey with pride.

8. Outcome
As all journeys reach an end, so your spiritual quest will reach its goal. Take heart from this rune, as it tells you where you will find yourself at the end of your quest.

FEE

AUTHORITY

CRYSTAL RUNES

> *"Wealth is a comfort to all,*
> *Yet shall with many be shared,*
> *If a man would hope to gain*
> *Great honour before his lord."*
>
> Anglo-Saxon Rune Poem, trans. Ella Mortimer.

ELLA MORTIMER

Possessions, captivity, domestic, slavery.

Fee is double edged, as it involves both the acquisition of wealth and the responsibility that goes along with it. Its original meaning of "cattle" reminds us of the rural life of the first farmers, where the size of your herd was an indication of affluence.

But the wealth came at a price. Cattle needed care and protection; they needed to be nurtured. They are a domesticated animal, living only to serve, providing meat and milk and skins for human comfort.

The farmer has control over his herd, doling out feed and providing shelter. In this vein, the image of cattle can also be extended to the people under the protection of their feudal lord. You might even be reminded of the slave trade, its victims regarded as little more than cattle to their masters.

Fee shows us that along with wealth comes authority and responsibility, and the rune poem reminds us that there is more honour in sharing your wealth than hording it all for yourself.

In the Scandinavian tradition, *Fee* indicates the power of wealth to sow discord. For how much wealth does one person really need? Is it not more admirable to use your wealth to feed those under your care? And when does the accumulation of wealth give way to simple greed?

Fee counsels you to take care of those who rely on you for sustenance and protection, to use your wealth for the greater good, rather than keep it all for yourself. Look to your family, nurture your household, and share what you have with those who really rely on you.

Stone: Onyx

Onyx is paired with *Fee* for its power to reinforce a sense of responsibility, by enhancing your inner strength. Onyx helps build self-confidence and the ability to act with determination to strive toward your goals. It sharpens your reasoning and supports assertiveness and a willingness to enforce order in times of dispute. Thus it helps strengthen those qualities most admired in a leader, giving you the power to act with fairness and authority.

Alternate Stones:
Moonstone, to strengthen inner knowledge.
Amethyst, to bring stillness and meditation.

RAW

FREEDOM

> "*A fierce beast with great horns,
> It uses its horns to fight.
> Very dangerous, it walks the moors,
> A splendid creature of might.*"
>
> *Anglo-Saxon Rune Poem,* trans. Ella Mortimer.

ELLA MORTIMER

Wild, untamed, elemental, abandonment, virility.

The wild ox, the traditional meaning of this rune, evokes the raw, untamed energy of the bull. With its big, powerful horns and vicious nature, this animal symbolises everything primal and wild.

It is an abandonment of all civilised behaviour, but not by going it alone. The lone bull is mighty, but at the head of his herd he becomes invincible.

A counterpoint to the previous rune, *Raw* can be seen as elemental power, virility and energy. Where *Fee* was responsibility, *Raw* is unrestrained freedom. Where *Fee* was the tame herd, *Raw* is the stampede.

As mentioned before, I have chosen in this book to follow the Anglo-Saxon rune poem for the names and interpretations. But in the Scandinavian rune poems that led to the Viking runes, *Raw* held a slightly different meaning.

The Icelandic poem paints an image of torrential rain, ruining the harvest and soaking the shepherd in the field. Though the literal meaning may be different, the message is the same; the raw, elemental power of nature.

The Norwegian poem mentions dross from bad iron, indicating something base or corrupted, and then gives an image of a deer running over frozen snow. This interpretation points to the power of nature to overcome adversity. In the deepest sense, this meaning is not so dissimilar after all.

In all cases, this rune points to raw, untamed nature, in all its glory and power. You hold that power too, and if you use that strength for good, people will follow you.

When you let go of the cares imposed by modern society and give yourself permission to be free, to find the virility of nature within yourself, there is no limit to what you can achieve.

Stone: Haematite

Haematite pairs well with this rune for its ability to bring out your inner strength, to instill a sense of vitality and physical health. It strengthens your elementary power to make it available when emergency strikes, encouraging traits needed for survival in adversity. To this end, haematite helps you balance modern day stresses and overcome fear of failure. In short, it helps release you from modern day cares to find your inner freedom.

Alternate Stones:
Bloodstone, for physical strength.
Abstract Jasper, for confidence and emotional strength.

THORN

CHAOS

> "Severely sharp, a thorn is evil,
> To any who takes hold of it;
> Extremely cruel to the man,
> Who would among them sit."

Anglo-Saxon Rune Poem, trans. Ella Mortimer.

ELLA MORTIMER

Brutality, evil, dark influences, sickness, confusion.

In Anglo-Saxon, *Thorn's* primary meaning is clear; something sharp that causes injury.

In the Viking tradition, this rune means a "Giant" who brings anguish to women, and is related to the god Thor. Perhaps this meaning grew from the sound of the name, taking the interpretation away from its origins, but nevertheless it leads to the same divination.

Thorn is a sharp, sudden attack, something that brings evil in its wake. Whether it is a simple prick from a rose or a thunderbolt from the god Thor, it is an unexpected act of brutality. And with brutality comes illness or dark influences, leading to chaos and confusion.

Later runic interpretations have given *Thorn* an association with evil, more specifically the devil or a demon. It is a Christianisation of the pagan god Thor, taken from the Scandinavian rune poems. But in a deeper sense, this is simply a personification of the dark, the chaos that follows the thunder.

The Anglo-Saxon poem gives warning. If you take hold of the thorn it will prick you; if you play with fire, you will get burned. But if you choose to take the dark side, and join the evil-doers, your punishment will be exponentially worse. Take heed of the warning, and think well on your chosen action; consider the consequences.

Stone: Rainbow Flourite

I have chosen flourite to pair with *Thorn* because of its calming properties, which bring with them an ability to sort through chaotic thoughts to find an inner equilibrium. It provides strength for solving problems by improving your ability to absorb information and gather ideas together to form an understanding, providing the power to overcome adversity. Flourite strengthens reasoning and analytical skills, helping to enforce order among the chaos.

Alternate Stones:
Onyx, for self control and analytical power.
Turquoise, to help control your own fate.

VOICE

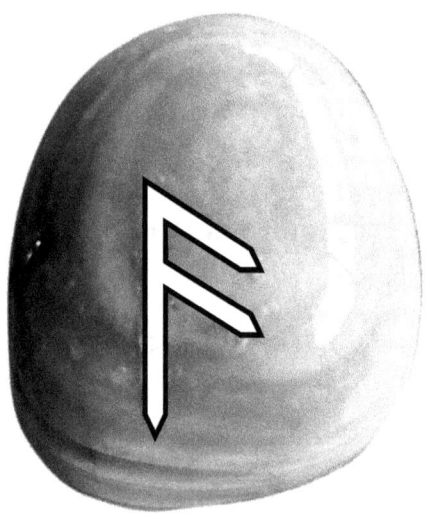

WISDOM

CRYSTAL RUNES

> *"Pillar of wisdom, font from whence*
> *All discourse doth arise,*
> *Every nobleman's pride and joy,*
> *And comfort to the wise."*

Anglo-Saxon Rune Poem, trans. Ella Mortimer.

ELLA MORTIMER

Divinity, good, messages, oracle, order, understanding.

Where *Thorn* is the onset of chaos, *Voice* is the voice of reason. In the Icelandic rune poem, *Voice* is equated with Odin, the lord of Valhalla. It is from this reference that this rune has become associated with God, or the voice of divine wisdom. The Norwegian poem describes this rune in two images: the first of a journey down an estuary; the second the sword in its scabbard. Perhaps the two images point toward the path you must take, something that guides the way.

Combining the three poems brings us to the concept of a guiding message, the knowledge needed to perform some task. Whether it is through the act of discourse to discover the truth, or a message from an oracle, or a simple signpost pointing out the path. In any case, this rune tells you to look for a sign, some message that will point the way.

The Anglo-Saxon poem describes the act of learning through discussion, an education usually only available to the nobleman, and a pursuit that brings wisdom to the learned man. In a world where knowledge was passed down through word of mouth in song, this is a potent image. The ability to communicate knowledge that sets us apart from animals.

Voice is asking you to be alert for some

message, a signal that will give knowledge, pointing toward the correct path. Be alert, and watch for signs. Use your analytical power to search for the knowledge you need to find your way. And trust your intuition, that divine voice within us all.

Stone: Banded Agate

This rune has been paired with Agate for its mind strengthening properties, to help you find the learning opportunities in all experiences. Agate helps with analytical problems, guiding you to find solutions through calm reasoning and rational thought. It is also believed to aid memory and assist recall of long forgotten events. It encourages contemplation and concentration, allowing you to absorb the lessons brought about by life's events.

Alternate Stones:
Amazonite, to align thought with intuition.
Moonstone, to open up to inner messages.

RIDE

JOURNEY

CRYSTAL RUNES

> *"To every warrior, riding is easy,*
> *When he doth rest in repose,*
> *But to he that sits over miles of road*
> *On a stout horse; very hard to those."*

Anglo-Saxon Rune Poem, trans. Ella Mortimer.

ELLA MORTIMER

Quest, travel, discovery, learning, adventure.

Traditionally, *Ride* denotes a journey or a quest, some sort of travel over long distance. It could mean a spiritual quest or a physical journey. An adventure or discovery, perhaps involving a lesson learnt.

All rune poems agree, this rune involves riding, though the Scandinavian record reminds us of the discomfort to the horse. The Anglo-Saxon poem speaks of pride also, the rider bragging of his prowess on a horse when he is sitting at home in comfort. And it points out that when a long journey is involved, travel is not such a pleasure. And it suggests that it is simple to plan, but a lot harder to put that plan into practice.

This rune suggests a journey, perhaps of some distance, with all the discomfort involved in such travel. If this is a spiritual journey, *Ride* warns that your quest may be long and difficult. It warns you not to be complacent about the ease of your travail, that it is easy to be confident before the journey starts, but that such things are more difficult in reality.

Take heed of the warning. Prepare for your journey with care and consideration, taking into account what you may need to make the ride more comfortable. Decide what is most necessary to make the journey a success.

Don't fall into the trap of planning and never actually doing. Do not enter into your quest with too much bravado, and remember the reality of what you face. Then, and only then, should you take the first step.

Stone: Yellow Calcite

Yellow Calcite is a stone of stimulation. It is paired with *Ride* for its power to overcome laziness and lack of motivation. It bestows energy and aids in development of ideas. Calcite gives you confidence to transform your ideas into action. It helps with positive thinking and the enthusiasm to follow a dream through to completion.

Alternate Stones:
Dalmation Jasper, to foster fearless adventure.
Mookaite, to balance thought with action.

CANDLE

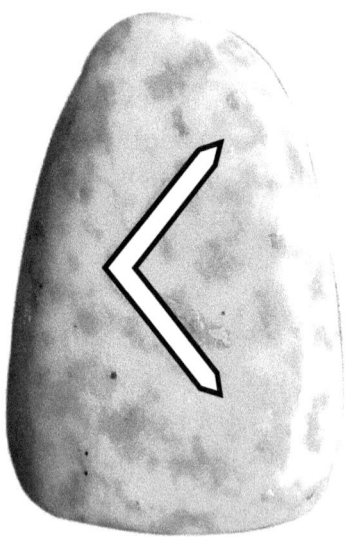

BEACON

CRYSTAL RUNES

> *"Pale and brilliant fire,*
> *To every living thing is known,*
> *Although it burns most often*
> *Where princes rest at home."*

Anglo-Saxon Rune Poem, trans. Ella Mortimer.

ELLA MORTIMER

Direction, hope, illumination, guiding light, map.

Candle is the beacon that leads the way. It lights the *Ride* with hope and points out the path. In the Viking rune poems, *Candle* means ulcer, a childhood illness, a fatal disease with painful spots. But perhaps the two meanings can be reconciled. The Anglo-Saxon image of fire lighting the home can be extended to include candle light, the solitary flame lighting the sick room. It is the fire that brings warmth and light, giving hope in the darkness.

Another aspect of fire is the bright light, the light at the end of the tunnel, or the white light of death. It signifies the end of travail, the light toward which we strive. It is a sign of comfort, brightening the dark places and leading the way.

Consider also, the power of fire. It can be a destructive force and yet it can be tamed. Something that would burn the forests and raze the fields can be brought inside and contained, to give warmth and light, to cook our food, to provide shelter from the cold. It is a sign of civilisation.

Consider this rune as a sign that there will be light. That the time of trouble will end and the sun will rise. Take comfort in the light of home, and remember that all distress can be tamed by right action.

Stone: Nephrite Jade

Nephrite is known as a healing stone, and a stone that protects. It is paired with *Candle* for its ability to dissolve doubt and encourage action. It can bring you out of a brooding state and into a state of peace. It helps in decision making and protects against hostility. It improves creativity and prepares you for the action required to complete your journey.

Alternate Stones:
Garnet, to relieve depression and give answers.
Tourmaline, to detoxify and relieve stress.

GIVE

GIVING

*"Honour and praise uplift a man
For worthy acts of charity,
And for the wretch with nothing,
He gains support and dignity."*

Anglo-Saxon Rune Poem, trans. Ella Mortimer.

ELLA MORTIMER

Offering, sacrifice, selflessness, helpfulness, the act of giving.

This rune extolls the virtue of giving. It is a gift freely given to one who is in need. *Give* is an act of charity with no thought to yourself. Some modern interpretations have twisted the meaning to suggest you might receive a gift, but that is erroneous, as the Anglo-Saxon poem clearly shows. This rune is not about getting, unless you are the wretch in need of support.

Consider this rune as an indication of sacrifice, of an act of charity that you will perform. Freely giving to others brings its own reward of honour and praise. Accept the thanks you receive as its own gift.

Give means an offering, from the heart, to those less fortunate. Never be afraid to give of yourself. You will be repaid in respect and self worth. It is an open exchange that brings loyalty and love. It is giving for the pure joy of giving, just as in a love match, where you give just because it makes your loved one happy, and you get the same in return.

Your soul will glow with the pleasure of seeing the gratitude of others. In giving of yourself, you strengthen bonds of friendship, build business prowess and gain partnerships in life and even love.

This rune is about building bridges,

through the gift of fortune which improves society and gives back a thousand fold. It is an investment of yourself that will grow just like any other investment. You have to give in order to receive.

Stone: Rose Quartz

Give is paired with rose quartz for its ability to make us gentle, while building resolve. It opens your soul to empathy and sensitivity, guiding you toward helpful action. It opens your heart to love, both of yourself and others, which allows kind action toward the people around you. It is a stone of gentle love that brings you closer to your fellow man and makes you feel their needs in a way that encourages you to express your love in charity toward others.

Alternate Stones:
Carnelian, fosters willingness to help.
Malachite, strengthens justice and empathy.

WIN

WINNING

CRYSTAL RUNES

> *"Happy is he who suffers little*
> *Of grief, illness or distress,*
> *And himself has abundant security,*
> *With constant bliss and success."*

Anglo-Saxon Rune Poem, trans. Ella Mortimer.

ELLA MORTIMER

Joy, attainment, receiving, gaining, success.

Win is the rune of joy, of happiness and success. It is the partner of *Give*; it is the rune of receiving. All suffering is gone, and there is only light. A rune of reward, of attainment, of gaining that which you most desire.

This a rune of outcomes, the longed for prize at the end of toil. The harvest after the long season of planting and growing. All of your troubles are cleared and you will bask in harmony and joy. All of your selfless acts, all of your hard work, will repay you now. Victory in the face of chaos, brought about by right action and selflessness.

The Anglo-Saxon rune poem points to the happiness of the rich; a life of comfort which knows no pain or trouble. But implicit between the lines is a reminder of the other side, of the person who does not have the same security.

It is a suggestion to remember that not everyone has the same luck, the same richness of life. When life is easy it is easy to be happy. It is easy to forget your troubles when you are in a moment of peace, and you should remember that good fortune can turn, so be grateful for your success and pay attention to those who need you.

It is wonderful to bask in the sun, but remember the path that brought you here.

Stone: Carnelian

Carnelian is said to bring optimism and joy, and it is for this reason that its rune is *Win*. Carnelian makes you steadfast and idealistic, giving you the strength to stand up for what is right. In this way it gives you the courage to overcome difficulties, and helps you to share your success with others.

Alternate Stones:
Red Jasper, to pursue and achieve your goals.
Aventurine, to make dreams come true.

HAIL

DISRUPTION

CRYSTAL RUNES

> *"Falling from heaven's clouds,*
> *Hail is the whitest of grain.*
> *Tossed about in gusts of wind,*
> *And then it turns to rain."*

Anglo-Saxon Rune Poem, trans. Ella Mortimer.

ELLA MORTIMER

Storm, destruction, the elements, disaster, force of nature.

Hail describes the sudden fury of a storm. Traditional divination texts ascribe the meaning of disruption or destruction, and this is certainly one interpretation. It also evokes the raw power of the elements, a force of nature over which we have no control.

All the rune poems are alike in their emphasis on the storm aspect and the image of hail as "white grain". The Anglo-Saxon poem turns the image about, showing that the hail may be ferocious as it falls, but it will melt into water.

Thus we are reminded of the transient nature of any misfortune. *Hail* is sudden misfortune, devastating in its power and the damage it can cause. But the storm will pass, and the trouble will eventually end.

This rune emphasises the need to take shelter, to ride out the storm, and wait until the calm before venturing forth to repair the damage.

The danger may be frightening at the time, but it will melt away when the storm is over. It is an event you cannot control, but you can decide what you will do to fix the damage afterwards.

Stone: Snowflake Obsidian

Snowflake obsidian, with its white spots in a glassy black matrix, is the perfect partner for *Hail*. But it is not only for its appearance that I chose this stone. Obsidian will strengthen your survival instinct while at the same time will calm fears and give a sense of security.

It helps dissolve pain and clears away negative influences. While the pure black form of the stone was used in paleolithic times to fashion weapons, it was later used to produce mirrors. A stone of violence was transmuted into a thing of beauty.

Alternate Stones:
Onyx, to clarify confusion and combat fears.
Tourmaline, to relieve stress and bring healing.

NEED

NECESSITY

CRYSTAL RUNES

*"Though it distresses the heart,
Help and healing comes of need,
If only the child of strife
Would at the earliest take heed."*

Anglo-Saxon Rune Poem, trans. Ella Mortimer.

ELLA MORTIMER

Endurance, suffering, constraint, persistence, perseverance.

Need is the complement of *Hail*. It is the hard work after the devastating storm. The Scandinavian rune poems emphasise the idea that we do what we have to do.

The Anglo-Saxon poem extends on this to warn that you should be strong when strife hits, and take action to fix what is causing the problem so that the healing can begin.

Need is constraint, in that we do what is necessary to rebuild and heal. It is endurance in the face of suffering, and persistence to keep at it until the strife is past.

It is the hard lesson, learnt through toil and pain. It is a reminder to keep striving, to be resilient and never give up in the face of adversity.

This rune suggests a need to be strong, to soldier on when times are difficult and events have laid you low.

Do not sit back and wait for help, although you should accept it when it is offered. Stand up and take on the challenge, take the first step on the long and difficult road to recovery, keep taking those steps one at a time, and build toward your own salvation.

Stone: Tiger Iron

Tiger Iron is the best stone for this rune because of its energising properties. It imparts strength to make changes in your life, to bring you into a new place of power.

It helps you find the most elegant solution to any problem and helps overcome apathy to get you moving on the road to new beginnings.

It provides endurance to overcome the difficulties that plague you, and helps lift your spirits so that you may take on the challenge with energetic enthusiasm.

Alternate Stones:
Amazonite, for determination to take charge.
Unakite, to calm anxiety and aid recovery.

ICE

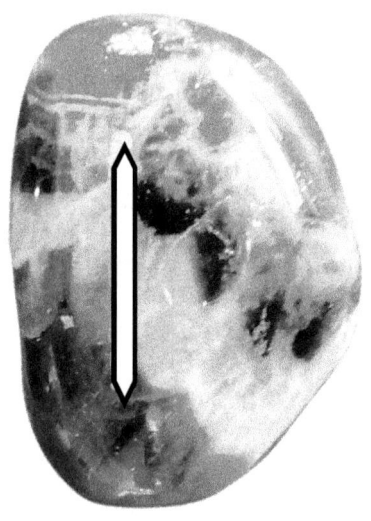

HIBERNATION

CRYSTAL RUNES

> *"Glistening clear as glass,*
> *Extremely slippery and cold,*
> *Jewel-like, a floor made of frost,*
> *A beautiful sight to behold."*

Anglo-Saxon Rune Poem, trans. Ella Mortimer.

Winter, standstill, changeless, impediment, waiting.

Ice is the deep cold of winter, when everything is at a standstill. The world is buried beneath snow and ice. The rivers are frozen over. Mother nature is in hibernation, waiting for the thaw.

It is silent, unmoving, and seemingly without life. But the ice glitters like diamonds, the white world breathtaking in its beauty. The Anglo-Saxon poem sees through the harsh cold to the stunning sight of a winter landscape.

This rune points to the standstill of winter, everything frozen in place. Now is not the time to act; it is a time of rest, of contemplation, of waiting for the spring.

Ice is a reminder to sit back and look, and see the beauty in the stillness. It is a time for meditation, for thinking and searching within. It tells us to look for the good, to find the silver lining.

There is good in every impediment. The ice reminds you to hold off, to delay action. There is good reason to wait, even if you cannot see it. Look deeper. Perhaps you are not ready, or perhaps the other influences in your life are not at optimum power. Perhaps there is a negative aspect that will damage your chance of success.

Take the time to stop and regroup, take

stock and wait for the right moment.

Stone: Amethyst

Amethyst has long been used to dispel bad dreams and enable peaceful sleep. It is a calming stone that aptly suits *Ice* for its ability to bring stillness to the mind. It aids in concentration and helps awaken your spiritual side. It heightens intuition and cultivates gentle, soothing thought. It is a perfect stone for bringing out your ability to melt away your blockages with calm, rational consideration.

Alternate Stones:
Blue Quartz, for calm and tranquillity.
Moonstone, for meditiation and inner intuition.

YEAR

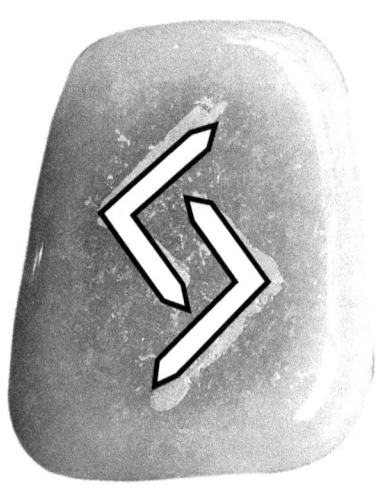

GROWTH

CRYSTAL RUNES

> "A year brings joy to the people,
> If holy heaven's king allows.
> The earth for rich and poor alike,
> Brings forth her shining boughs."

Anglo-Saxon Rune Poem, trans. Ella Mortimer.

ELLA MORTIMER

Change, result, reward, reaping, fertile, one year.

Where *Ice* is the frozen winter, *Year* is the summer harvest. The thaw has come, and the seed has sprouted forth in vigorous growth to bring its fruitful bounty.

The earth has come back to life, the waiting is over and the richness of nature bursts forth in all its glory. It is the end of the long year of work, and a celebration of life through the gifts of mother earth.

The earthly cycle of one year represents the completion of hard work. The toil of planting seeds and tending crops, the waiting for the plants to bear fruit, has all led to the harvest.

The poem reminds us that the earth's bounty is not always certain, but with hard work and good luck the outcome will be fortunate for one and all.

You will reap what you have sown, your hard work has paid off. Now is the time to enjoy the fruits of your labour. The difficult winter is past, the summer is in full bloom and you will have your reward.

But always remember it has come at a cost, and without the power of the universe on your side, you could not have reached this point. Your toil has paid off and now mother earth feeds her children in joy.

Stone: Green Aventurine

Aventurine's rich green colour glitters with the kiss of the sun. It matches *Year* in its celebration of earth's gifts, by increasing your ability to make your dreams come true. It brings enthusiasm and regeneration. It allows rebirth through its calming influence, which gives the ability to relax and recover, thus bringing on a renewal of spirit.

Alternate Stones:
Yellow Jasper, for endurance to pursue goals.
Amazonite, for determination to take charge.

BOW

VIGILANCE

> "*A hard tree, rough on the outside,*
> *Fixed firmly within the soil,*
> *With roots twisted underneath,*
> *Keeper of fire, and homeland's joy.*"
>
> *Anglo-Saxon Rune Poem,* trans. Ella Mortimer.

Defence, avertive, alert, watchful, caution, poison, retreat, on guard.

The original meaning of this rune is yew, indicating the yew tree. Branches of the yew tree were often used to craft powerful bows for hunting and defence. The Icelandic and Norwegian rune poems both mention its use to make bows.

Amulets of yew wood were thought to protect from harmful influences. The magic of yew wood was heightened by its crackling way of burning, and the Anglo-Saxon poem alludes to this, as does the Norwegian poem. The Anglo-Saxon dwells on the characteristic strength of the tree, hard and powerful and well rooted.

Yew trees were planted in graveyards in the belief that they would keep the souls of the dead contained, and for this reason, this rune has been associated with death. But more correctly, the use of the tree in burial grounds would have been protective in nature, keeping evil influences at bay.

In all these aspects, *Bow* is a rune that protects. A bow made of yew wood fires arrows at attackers. An amulet made of yew keeps bad spirits away. And trees of yew defended the sanctity of the dead. It is a rune of vigilance, of keeping yourself on guard against attack.

Emulate the protective power of this rune,

and find your inner strength to repel harmful influences. You have the strength to avert danger, to send the darkness away with the crackling fire of your own determination.

Stone: Rhodonite

Rhodonite has the power to repel negative influences, thus making it an excellent partner for this rune. It strengthens your ability to dissolve conflict through constructive collaberation. Rhodonite helps you stay clear and focused in times of stress or danger. Its power to instill calm in the face of attack will help you to solve problems peacefully and without fear.

Alternate Stones:
Bloodstone, for equilibrium and strength.
Crazy Lace Agate, protects from negative energy.

PEAR

INDULGENCE

> *"Feasting, games and laughter,*
> *For proud warriors all,*
> *Where they sit in happiness,*
> *Together in the beer hall."*
>
> Anglo-Saxon Rune Poem, trans. Ella Mortimer.

ELLA MORTIMER

Luxury, intoxication, sensuality, pleasure, unrestrained, chance.

Where *Bow* is vigilance, *Pear* is pleasure. The true meaning of this rune is much contested, interpreted variously as "apple", or "dice cup", or "mystery", or even "mountain". The source for this discrepancy is a gap in the text of the Anglo-Saxon rune poem, whereby the one-word meaning of the rune is missing.

The most commonly accepted meaning of "dice cup" comes from an old interpretation that supposed the symbol for this rune resembled some kind of cup, and that the games and laughter described in the poem must involve gambling. The arbitrary nature of this assumption is pure speculation.

The next most popular meaning is "apple". Introduced to Britain by the Romans, apples and pears were used in Saxon times to make cider. Its name could have evolved from the Roman word for pear, "pyrus", or could be related to the Anglo-Saxon word for beer, "beor".

Apples figure in many ancient myths and have a long history as the fruit of lovers, whether eaten by Persian brides, a romantic token in ancient Greece, or an after dinner aphrodisiac at Roman feasts. In Roman cookbooks, apples and pears are interchangeable, and in fact pears were preferred for their sweetness. In Homer, pears are a "gift of the gods". They were used to make pear wine from Roman times, a beverage later dubbed "Perry" in the court of Henry VIII.

The runes described in Tacitus were carved on twigs from a fruit-bearing tree, most likely an apple tree. Many runes take their names from trees. It is not a great leap that there would be a rune named for the actual tree from which the runes were fashioned. Whether sumptuously prepared for the banquet table, or imbibed as pear wine, this fruit aptly fits the meaning suggested in the Anglo-Saxon rune poem.

Pear is about abandonment, unrestrained sensuality, and intoxication. It is a rune of pleasure, of feasting with friends and family, and of celebration. It is a release from worldly cares, a suggestion to indulge and take a chance, to forget your worries for a while and simply have fun. Give in to the luxury of pure indulgence and bask in the joy of life.

Stone: Malachite

Malachite is matched with *Pear* for its power to enhance sensuality and appreciation of beauty. It encourages empathy and removes inhibitions, helping you to express your feelings without shyness. It increases imagination, and has the ability to resolve sexual problems.

Alternate Stones:
Opal, for spontaneity, expression and passion.
Red Jasper, for enjoyment and sexual passion.

SHIELD

RETREAT

CRYSTAL RUNES

> *"The sedge grows on the water,*
> *Most often in the marsh.*
> *It grimly wounds, it burns the blood,*
> *Of one who dares to grasp."*

Anglo-Saxon Rune Poem, trans. Ella Mortimer.

ELLA MORTIMER

Taking care, warding off, beware, protection, alertness, take cover.

The Anglo-Saxon rune poem paints an image of sedge grass growing in the water and gives warning of its sword-like fronds, which will inflict vicious lacerations if you try to pull it out of its marshy bed. The rune name is related to the word for Elk and by extension Elk-sedge.

The traditional interpretation of this rune is defence. The translation of *Shield* is a nod to this, but it is defence in the form of taking care, of being aware, rather than hiding behind a shield in the literal sense. It is a warning to retreat, rather than surge forward into danger.

The sedge will not harm you if you leave it be. It is only when you reach out to pluck the grass that you cause injury to yourself. The rune poem warns to leave things alone, to stand back and avoid danger, rather than face it head on.

The message of *Shield* is to let sleeping dogs lie. Don't go looking for trouble or you will get hurt. Take care of yourself, provide your own protection, through careful consideration of the consequences of your actions.

Don't march out into danger without taking care to prevent injury. Wear a shield of alertness, be ready to take cover, and step out of danger.

CRYSTAL RUNES

Stone: Heliotrope

Heliotrope is paired with *Shield* for its ability to strengthen your own protective power. The red splotches in the green stone give it the alternative name of "bloodstone", and are an apt reminder of the blood drawn by the sedge reeds of the rune poem.

It helps you shield yourself from harm by calming impatience and neutralising aggressive impulses. Heliotrope helps you keep control in the face of unexpected attack, allowing you to adjust quickly and take cover.

Alternate Stones:
Abstract Jasper, protects from falsehood.
Tiger Eye, to overcome difficult situations.

SIGNAL

ADVANCE

> *"The sun brings feasting and joy,*
> *When seafarers choose to wend*
> *Over the fish's bath until*
> *They bring their ship to land."*
>
> *Anglo-Saxon Rune Poem,* trans. Ella Mortimer.

ELLA MORTIMER

Solar ray, life force, power of the sun, positive movement, going forth.

Signal is the power of the sun, the guiding light for navigators. The Anglo-Saxon poem talks of the good fortune of clear skies, which allows the sun to shine through and guide them to land.

The Scandinavian poems also talk of the sun, its light blessing the world and melting the ice. It is the opposite of *Shield*, telling you there is no more need to be cautious, to step out into the sunlight and be guided by the sun's golden rays.

Signal reminds us of the power of sunlight, a positive force in the universe. It shines forth to vanquish the darkness, and it causes mother nature to thrive. It brings energy and healing, and offers guidance in the form of hope and direction. But sunlight is an uncompromising force, blinding and burning if its power is taken for granted. Traditional interpretations emphasise the harsh nature of the sun. It is the bright white light that can burn or give life.

This rune is giving a positive message of hope. It tells you to go forth with confidence, secure in your triumph over adversity. But never forget the raw power of this gift.

Remember to respect the force that hands you this victory, for it could just as easily have destroyed, rather than helped.

Stone: Citrine

Citrine is a beautiful yellow quartz, its golden light evocative of the sun that gives this rune its name. It bestows courage to face the world, and encourages a desire to experience new things. It pulls you out of depression and helps strengthen your joy of life. It warms the body, gives confidence, and stimulates a sense of adventure.

Alternate Stones:
Yellow Calcite, to energise and overcome fear.
Tiger Iron, to strengthen impulse for change.

TRY

FIGHTING

CRYSTAL RUNES

> "Courage is a trait that holds
> Faith with princes well,
> And as they journey through the dark
> Of night, it will never fail."

Anglo-Saxon Rune Poem, trans. Ella Mortimer.

ELLA MORTIMER

Battle, courage, ability, perseverence, victory, strength.

Related to the god Tiw, this rune represents the courage of the warrior. Tiw was equated with the Roman god Mars, the god of war, and is the origin of the word Tuesday.

Where the Ango-Saxon poem talks of courage and persistence through the dark of night, the Scandinavian poems link it directly with the one-armed god, who offered his hand to the wolf Fenrir, to be taken in its jaws so that it might be bound.

The Anglo-Saxon rune poem paints the image of a brave prince setting forth into the dark. It tells you that courage serves you well in even the worst situations.

It is the ability to conquer fear, to never give up even when hope seems gone. Even the bravest warrior feels fear, but it is his determination to press on in spite of the danger that makes him brave.

Try is a rune of strength and soldiering on, sticking to it no matter what stands in your way. It is a promise of victory, of triumph over adversity. It tells you that a warrior can win through any battle with courage and a steady heart.

Just as Tiw pressed forward and, through courageous self-sacrifice, won the day, so too can you triumph over your foes. This rune advises you to keep fighting, to continue your quest with courage and willingness to do anything to get to your goal. Never give up.

Stone: Red Jasper

Red Jasper is a stone of courage, helping you to overcome fear and anxiety and giving you the strength to step forward. Jasper brings out your warrior nature, strengthening your determination to reach your goal. It is paired with *Try* to help you realise your power to face any task and take action without fear.

Alternate Stones:
Haematite, for courage and survival instinct.
Amazonite, to dissolve apprehension.

BIRTH

LOVING

CRYSTAL RUNES

*"A tree without shoots, bears fruitless twigs
On radiant branches high.
Loaded with leaves, its fair crown
Rises toward the sky."*

Anglo-Saxon Rune Poem, trans. Ella Mortimer.

ELLA MORTIMER

Growth, new beginnings, rebirth, awakening, passion.

As *Try* evoked the warrior, *Birth* is the image of life. *Try* taught us to do battle, while *Birth* brings the dawn after the dark night. The rune poems all talk of the birch tree, which reaches its bare branches to the sky and bursts forth with new leaves in the spring.

Taking this image to its divinatory conclusion, this rune is often associated with rebirth, or new beginnings. The branches may be bare, but they are radiant, reaching high in triumph. Then the new birth brings leaves to fill those branches with beautiful life.

It is a celebration of spring, a triumph of rebirth, and a benediction to the glory of nature, which rises from the winter again and again. It is an awakening that dispels the dark and brings forth passion for life. It is mother nature at her most fertile, her most creative, her most beautiful.

Birth is showing you new life, the new beginning ready to surround you with the bloom of spring's new growth. The slow passage through darkness is over, and now you will see a burst of rapid growth, sudden and glorious.

A period of great fertility and regenerative power is upon you. Fill your heart with the positive energy of rebirth, and take the chance to enter the new life with joy.

Stone: Unakite

The stone of rebirth, Unakite is a perfect partner for *Birth*. Unakite helps you develop a positive self-image, which allows for constructive growth in the sense of a spiritual rebirth. It helps stabilise emotion to facilitate regeneration after a time of stress or pain. It supports healing, builds strength, and opens the heart to new life.

Alternate Stones:
Aventurine, for personal growth, regeneration.
Moss Agate, for abundance and balance.

WAY

VEHICLE

CRYSTAL RUNES

*"Proud of hoof, with heroes around,
A joy for warriors and princes.
On horseback the wealthy exchange words;
A horse will comfort the restless."*

Anglo-Saxon Rune Poem, trans. Ella Mortimer.

ELLA MORTIMER

Movement, progress, the means, mode of travel, transport.

Way means the horse, used to signify movement or travel, or more correctly, transport. As the rune poem suggests, the horse is a symbol of status, and a chance for people to meet and talk as they ride, and it will carry the restless person on their next journey. So not only does it facilitate travel, but it brings people together, as companions along the way.

In our modern world, the nearest equivalent would be the family car. A vehicle which carries us from place to place, in which we can talk and enjoy each other's company as we ride. It even carries a similar element of status, as the rich might show their wealth in the car they drive.

In a practical sense, this rune indicates the means, the way by which you achieve your goal. It is the mode by which you achieve progress in your chosen direction. It is the companions you take with you, whether they are friends and family or the more spiritual companions of thought and emotion. It is the whole package of embarking on a journey that will take you toward a new place.

Way indicates travel or development, a move toward something. It may be a spiritual journey or it may be physical travel. You are embarking on an adventure, with good friends and a reliable vehicle, with hope and good intentions.

Stone: Sodalite

Paired with *Way*, is Sodalite, a beautiful blue stone with white veins. It is not generally associated with travel, but it does encourage idealism and a personal drive. It helps you accept your life choices and brings you to an acceptance of yourself. It instills a sense of longing for freedom and the open road. It helps you remove those things that block your forward progress, and in this way it provides an opening to start you on your journey.

Alternate Stones:
Crazy Lace Agate, for serenity and protection.
Mookaite, to inspire new experiences.

MAN

DRIVER

CRYSTAL RUNES

*"A man of mirth is loved by his son,
But each shall the other betray.
For the lord will doom his wretched flesh;
Entrust it to the earth to decay."*

Anglo-Saxon Rune Poem, trans. Ella Mortimer.

ELLA MORTIMER

The rider, the self, the method, traveller, controller.

Man has long been associated with the self or the human race. In the purest sense, it is the cycle of life and death, as indicated in the Scandinavian poems which emphasise a man's relation to the dust from whence he came.

The Anglo-Saxon poem reminds us of the end of life, returning to that dust. But it also extols the love of a son for his father despite the inevitable betrayal of death.

This rune reminds us that we control our fate, that we may live life to the full, even if that life will eventually be taken from us. It is our choice how we live our lives while they last.

It is in this aspect that *Man* is the partner of *Way*. *Man* is the rider of the horse, the driver of the car, the leader of the company of travellers. *Man* is the one in control of his life.

Human life is fragile and short. All of us are mortal, with no control over the moment of our death. So in this there is a warning, that all good things come to an end.

Enjoy the journey while it lasts, and do not fear the end to come. Take each moment for itself, and share love and good times with your family and friends. Take charge of the journey, lead yourself along the path and take the time to live life to the fullest.

CRYSTAL RUNES

Stone: Clear Quartz

Clear Quartz is the stone of inner clarity, of awareness of your inner self. For this reason, it is paired with *Man*. Quartz helps you realise your own path, and encourages trust in yourself. It allows you to strengthen your own belief and leads you to go your own way. It encourages a deep knowledge of self, enabling the ability to step forward with confidence that your path is right for you.

Alternate Stones:
Turquoise, to strengthen self knowledge.
Onyx, to bring inner peace and clarity.

LAGOON

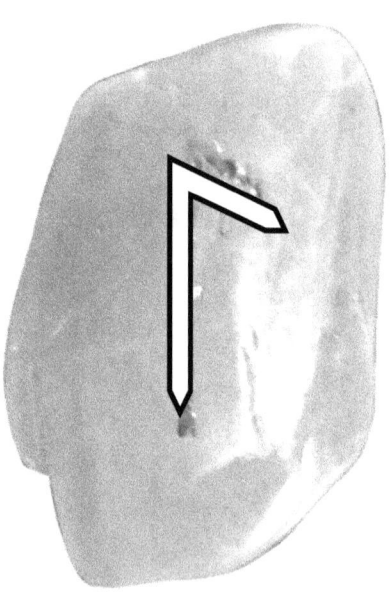

PREPARATION

CRYSTAL RUNES

*"The water seems endless to the person,
Who ventures out in a vessel unstable.
The waves can be very frightening,
When the sea-steed refuses its bridle."*

Anglo-Saxon Rune Poem, trans. Ella Mortimer.

ELLA MORTIMER

Hidden danger, illusions, be prepared, test the waters.

Lagoon is not still water, but quite the opposite. Although the name might suggest a quiet body of water, it is an illusion. A lagoon is a lake with an outlet to the sea. It is at this point that the current can be the most dangerous, and the waves most perilous.

Beneath the water are all manner of hidden dangers, rendered invisible by the disturbance at the surface. Perhaps it is this aspect of water that has led to traditional interpretations of the human power of intuition. They suggest an attempt to see beneath the surface.

All the rune poems give an image of rushing water, moving in eddies and waterfalls and ocean waves. But the Anglo-Saxon poem gives hope, by warning of the danger. Between the lines is a suggestion that we should see to our vessel, make sure the ship is sea-worthy before we venture out onto the churning water.

So *Lagoon* is a rune of being prepared. Of venturing forth only when everything is in good order. It counsels that a disaster would be of your own making. If you go to sea in a leaky boat, it's your own fault if that boat sinks beneath the waves. Take the time to set your house in order, maintain your vessel with care, and set out only when you are sure your journey will proceed in safety.

CRYSTAL RUNES

Stone: Moonstone

The stone of the moon that controls the tides, Moonstone is apt for the rune of water. Although it is generally associated with intuition, it also strengthens your ability to see the danger and calm your impulse to react. It this way it helps prepare you for the task ahead. It helps you look inside to see the hidden dangers before you venture out.

Alternate Stones:
Banded Agate, for contemplation and thought.
Blue Quartz, for tranquillity and creativity.

SPRING

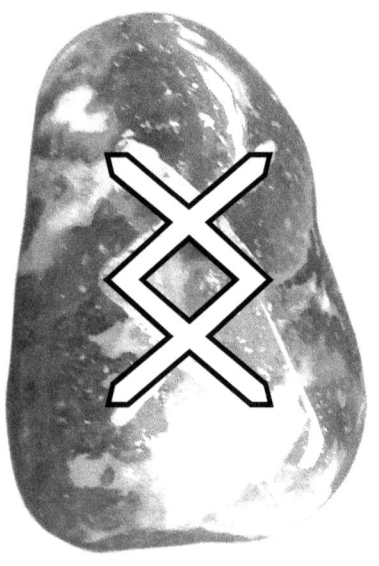

COMPLETION

> *"Ing was first among the East Danes,*
> *Seen by men until he went again,*
> *Over the waves after his chariot,*
> *Thus the princes named the brave man."*

Anglo-Saxon Rune Poem, trans. Ella Mortimer.

ELLA MORTIMER

Fertility, new life, passage, regeneration, liminality.

The god Ing was a legendary hero, believed to be the progenitor of the Saxon people. He is associated with fertility and domestic prosperity. The Anglo-Saxon rune poem describes his departure from the land, following his chariot over the waves, and remembers him for his bravery.

It is an image of the end of life, and embarking on the last journey, leaving loved-ones behind. But in his role as a fertility god, it does not mean death. Death is just an ending, and a new beginning is just around the corner.

Spring is a rune of new life and new beginnings. But more than that, it is a completion of a cycle, an end to the old life in readiness for the new. Where *Lagoon* was the preparation and the perilous journey, *Spring* is the end of the road, the conclusion of that journey. Now is the time to leave the old life behind.

Spring is a rune of passage, that moment between one life and the next, and the act of stepping through. It is the end of a journey, a goal achieved, and a place to stop and rest. It is the beginning of a new journey, leading to a new life in another place.

In the purest sense, *Spring* is regeneration. It is not the full growth of new life, but rather the seed, the potential not yet realised. The bud about to burst. It is a moment of pause between one journey and the next, standing right in the doorway, one foot in each world.

Look on this rune as an indication that your time of travail is done. You have reached the end of a cycle, the finish line, the goal for which you have striven until now. Take a deep breath and look ahead, to see what lies in wait. Then step forward, into something new.

Stone: Moss Agate

Moss Agate is a stone that brings new ideas, removes old blockages and allows new movement. Its ability to promote regeneration gives it an affinity with the rune of *Spring*. It helps you move forward to new things by bringing inspiration and removing stress and fear. It clears away the old thought processes to promote recovery and bring in fresh new life.

Alternate Stones:
Green Jasper, to calm fears and revitalise.
Rutilated Quartz, for movement and energy.

ETHOS

HISTORY

CRYSTAL RUNES

> *"Home is much loved by every man,*
> *If he may often possess,*
> *That which is right and proper,*
> *In his splendid house."*

Anglo-Saxon Rune Poem, trans. Ella Mortimer.

ELLA MORTIMER

Inheritance, family, home, connection to place, lifetime.

Ethos signifies all that we hold sacred about home, place and heritage. As the Anglo-Saxon rune poem suggests, this rune is about the love of home that comes when everything is in order. This includes that sense of what is culturally correct, and takes into account the idea of what makes a comfortable home.

Over the years, this rune has come to mean a sense of belonging to a place and a people, and a connection to the history of that place and people. The rune poem perhaps does not go that far, but it is there between the lines. For that which is right and proper could encompass all of that.

Ethos is the soil beneath our feet, the hearth that heats our home, the stories that colour our past, and the comfort that blesses our rest.

The poem gives the image of doing right by your house, which includes your people and your place; of providing what is necessary for a good life.

Take this rune as an indication that now is a time to set affairs to right and see to the health of your family.

Put your house in order to ensure the comfort and security of all you hold dear. Now is not a time to be off adventuring or spending too much time at work.

Take a break, and use the time to reconnect with house and home.

Stone: Fossilised Wood

Ethos has been paired with Fossilised Wood, which reminds us of the permanence of nature. It helps us feel connected with the earth and rooted in place. The fact that a living tree can eventually become one with the stones of the earth, shows us how the way we live today can become set in history tomorrow, how the society we create becomes the inheritance of our children.

Alternate Stones:
Dalmation Jasper, to connect with loved ones.
Rhyolite, for connection to the earth.

DAY

TODAY

CRYSTAL RUNES

> "**Sent by the lord, dear to man,**
> **Pure light of the creator,**
> **Mirth and hope, useful to all,**
> **Alike both prosperous and poor.**"
>
> *Anglo-Saxon Rune Poem,* trans. Ella Mortimer.

ELLA MORTIMER

The moment, daily life, one day, living in the present.

Where *Ethos* is the history of place, *Day* is the path of the sun, the moment of today. The rune poem is a celebration of the sun, which lights the world, gives hope and happiness, gives warmth and helps the crops to grow, and never discriminates between rich and poor. Every one and every thing on this planet is nurtured by the sun.

Day is a symbol of prosperity, a fruitful moment fuelled by light from the sun. Every day the sun returns, watching over us as we work, rest and play. It does not yearn for tomorrow, or regret yesterday. It lives in the moment, day to day, until all those days add up to the *Ethos* of place and people.

This rune is reminding you to live in the moment. Enjoy the day for what it is, without worrying about what is to come. Live life to the fullest, without wishing for something you have lost. No pining for the past, no yearning for the future.

Experience each day in the present, and never miss a moment. Life is there to be lived, and if you spend your days thinking of other times you will not see it passing by. Don't miss out on the wonder of life all around you.

Don't miss your children growing, or your own parents growing old. Be present for yourself and your family. Stop chasing the future and live for today.

Stone: Chalcedony

Blue Chalcedony is known for its power to bring a feeling of peace. Its ability to encourage simple pleasure in the people and animals in your life makes it a perfect partner for Day. It makes you carefree, lightens your heart and makes you optimistic about life. Use this stone to open your mind to possibilities, to be creative and responsive to the everyday world around you.

Alternate Stones:
Clear Quartz, for balance and perception.
Sodalite, for inner peace and balance.

QUICK KEY

Physical	Emotional	Spiritual
FEE Authority Onyx	 **HAIL** Disruption Snowflake Obsidian	**TRY** Fighting Red Jasper
RAW Freedom Haematite	 **NEED** Necessity Tiger Iron	**BIRTH** Loving Unakite
 **THORN** Chaos Flourite	 **ICE** Hibernation Amethyst	 **WAY** Vehicle Sodalite
 **VOICE** Wisdom Agate	 **YEAR** Growth Aventurine	**MAN** Driver Clear Quartz
 **RIDE** Journey Calcite	**BOW** Vigilance Rhodonite	 **LAGOON** Preparation Moonstone
 **CANDLE** Beacon Nephrite	**PEAR** Indulgence Malachite	**SPRING** Completion Moss Agate
 **GIVE** Giving Rose Quartz	**SHIELD** Retreat Bloodstone	**ETHOS** History Fossilised Wood
WIN Winning Carnelian	**SIGNAL** Advance Citrine	**DAY** Today Chalcedony

OTHER WORKS BY ELLA MORTIMER

Historical Novel:
The Curse of Mycenae

Fantasy Series, The Race of Fire:
Revealing Rexa
Awakening Sand
Rekindling Truth

Other Fantasy Works:
Kiss of Kelloree (A Novelette)
Wired Out (A Novella)
Coming Soon
The Temple Beautiful

Poetry:
Beneath the Sea (An Anthology)

Check Out Ella's Website:
theraceoffire.amentibooks.com

Join Ella on Facebook:
www.facebook.com/EllaMortimerAuthor

www.ingramcontent.com/pod-product-compliance
Lightning Source LLC
LaVergne TN
LVHW051603070426
835507LV00021B/2732